HANDS-ON SCIENCE PROJECTS

PHYSICS

FIND OUT ABOUT LEVERS, MAGNETS AND MOTORS WITH 50 GREAT EXPERIMENTS AND PROJECTS

CHRIS OXLADE

southwater

This edition is published by Southwater, an imprint of
Anness Publishing Ltd, Hermes House, 88–89 Blackfriars Road,
London SE1 8HA; tel. 020 7401 2077; fax 020 7633 9499

www.southwaterbooks.com; www.annesspublishing.com

If you like the images in this book and would like to investigate
using them for publishing, promotions or advertising,
please visit our website www.practicalpictures.com
for more information.

UK agent: The Manning Partnership Ltd;
tel. 01225 478444; fax 01225 478440;
sales@manning-partnership.co.uk
UK distributor: Grantham Book Services Ltd;
tel. 01476 541080; fax 01476 541061;
orders@gbs.tbs-ltd.co.uk
North American agent/distributor: National Book Network;
tel. 301 459 3366; fax 301 429 5746; www.nbnbooks.com
Australian agent/distributor: Pan Macmillan Australia;
tel. 1300 135 113; fax 1300 135 103;
customer.service@macmillan.com.au
New Zealand agent/distributor:
David Bateman Ltd; tel. (09) 415 7664;
fax (09) 415 8892

Publisher: Joanna Lorenz
Managing Editor: Linda Fraser
Editors: Jennifer Schofield and Clare Gooden
Production Controller: Steve Lang
Contributing Authors: John Farndon, Jen Green,
Robin Kerrod, Chris Oxlade, Steve Parker, Rodney Walshaw
Designer: Axis Design Editions Ltd
Photographers: Paul Bricknell, John Freeman, Don Last,
Robert Pickett, Tim Ridley
Illustrators: Cy Baker/Wildlife Art, Stephen Bennington,
Peter Bull Art Studio, Stuart Carter, Simon Gurr, Richard Hawke,
Nick Hawken, Michael Lamb, Alan Male/Linden Artists,
Guy Smith, Clive Spong, Stephen Sweet/Simon Girling and
Associates, Alisa Tingley, John Whetton
Stylists: Ken Campbell, Jane Coney, Marion Elliot, Tim Grabham,
Thomasina Smith, Isolde Sommerfeldt, Melanie Williams

ETHICAL TRADING POLICY
Because of our ongoing ecological investment programme,
you, as our customer, can have the pleasure and reassurance
of knowing that a tree is being cultivated on your behalf to
naturally replace the materials used to make the book you are
holding. For further information about this scheme, go to
www.annesspublishing.com/trees

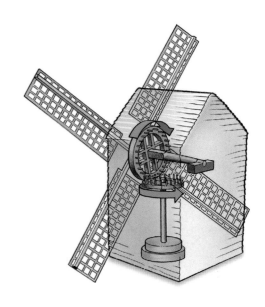

Previously published as *Hands-On Science: Physics*

PUBLISHER'S NOTE
The publishers have made every effort to ensure that all instructions
contained within this book are accurate and safe, and cannot accept
liability for any resulting injury, damage or loss to persons or property,
however they may arise.

Contents

Physical and Material Marvels

We live in a world of engineering marvels—of soaring tower blocks, wide-spanning bridges and massive dams. We can communicate with almost everyone, anywhere on the Earth, and even in Space. This book shows the part that science and technology have played in setting the pace of change. Science accumulates knowledge about the world by observation, study and experiment. Technology puts the knowledge into practical use as inventions to improve the quality of life.

Chemical change

Over the past 100 years, scientists have invented many substances, such as plastics, medicines, and detergents, that we take for granted today. These substances are created by chemical reactions. In a chemical reaction, a new substance (called a product) is made as a result of other substances (called reactants) undergoing chemical change. Many chemical reactions happen naturally, such as oil (gasoline) and gas, which form from the remains of animals and plants. They are called hydrocarbons, because they are mixtures of hydrogen and carbon.

The following experiments demonstrate the three main ways in which chemical reactions can happen—by passing electricity through substances, by heating them, or simply by mixing them together. In the first, electricity breaks down salty water to make chlorine (the disinfectant often used in swimming pools). In the second, heat turns sugar, which is made from carbon, hydrogen, and oxygen, into pure carbon. Finally, you make the gas used in some fire extinguishers by mixing bicarbonate of soda and vinegar together.

▲ **Checking up**
A technician is ensuring all the bottles of chemicals are correctly labeled. Accuracy is very important in science.

YOU WILL NEED

Electrolysis: battery (4–6 volts), bulb and holder, wires, wire strippers, screwdriver, paper clips, salt, jar, water.

Heat changes: old pan, teaspoon, sugar, stove.

Getting a reaction: teaspoon, bicarbonate of soda, glass bowl, vinegar, matches.

How oil is formed

The story of oil begins in warm seas full of living things. As they die, they fall to the bottom of the sea floor to decay into thick, black mud.

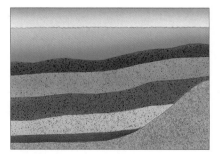

In time, mud is buried beneath many layers of sand, with clay in between. The sediments (deposits) sink deeper and deeper, and also become hotter.

After millions of years, the sediments fold under pressure. Oil from the black mud is forced into sandstones and trapped under the layers of clay.

Electrolysis

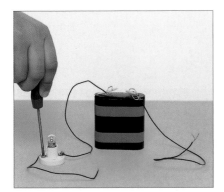

I Connect the battery and bulb holder with wires, as shown here. Remove ½in of insulation from each end of wire. Use the paper clips to attach the wires to the battery.

2 Stir salt into a jar of water until no more dissolves. Dip the two bare wire ends into the mixture and hold them about ½in apart. Look for bubbles forming around them.

3 The bulb should light to show that electricity is passing through. Carefully sniff the jar from 8in away. What does it smell like? The smell is like swimming pools!

Heat changes

I Make sure the pan is completely dry. Spread one teaspoonful of sugar across the bottom of the pan. Aim for a thin layer—about ¼in thick.

2 Place the pan on the stove and set to low heat. After a few minutes, the sugar will start to melt into a thick, brown liquid. You may begin to see a few wisps of steam.

3 The sugar starts to bubble as it breaks down and gives off steam. If you continue heating the sugar, the brown, sticky liquid will change to solid black carbon.

Getting a reaction

The gas is called carbon dioxide. Ask an adult to lower a lighted match into the bowl. The flame goes out when it meets the gas.

I Place three heaped spoonfuls of bicarbonate of soda in the bowl. Cooks often add this white powder to vegetables, such as peas and carrots. It helps to keep their natural colour.

2 Carefully pour vinegar into the bowl. As the liquid mixes with the bicarbonate of soda, a chemical reaction happens. The mixture bubbles as a gas is given off.

Tests with yeast

For thousands of years, people all over the world have used yeast for brewing beer and baking bread. Yeast is a type of fungus that lives on the skins of many fruits. Just a spoonful of yeast contains millions of separate, single-celled (very simple) organisms. Each one works like a tiny chemical factory, taking in sugar, and giving out alcohol and carbon dioxide gas. While they feed, the yeast cells grow larger and then reproduce by splitting in half.

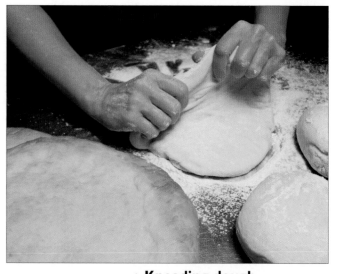

▲ Kneading dough
Bread is kneaded into a soft dough and then left in a warm place to rise. The dough is then kneaded again before it is baked. This process makes the yeast produce as many bubbles of gas as possible, so that the bread is light.

Yeast turns grape juice into alcoholic wine, and makes beer from mixtures of grain and water. When it is added to uncooked dough, yeast produces gas bubbles that make the bread light and soft. Brewing and baking are important modern industries that depend on yeast working quickly.

This project consists of four separate experiments. By comparing the results, you can discover the best conditions for yeast to grow. It needs a moist environment to be active. Lack of moisture makes the cells dry out and hibernate (sleep). Add water to dried, powdered yeast, and—even after many years—it will become active again.

Finding the best conditions

YOU WILL NEED

measuring cup, water, kettle, adhesive colored labels, four small glass jars, teaspoon, dried yeast granules, sugar, scissors, plastic wrap, three rubber bands, two heatproof bowls, ice cubes.

1 Half fill a kettle with water. Ask an adult to boil it for you, and then put it aside to cool. Boiling the water kills all living organisms that might stop the yeast from growing.

2 Label the glass jars, one to four. Put a level teaspoonful of dried yeast into each jar as shown here. Then put the same amount of sugar into each jar.

3 Pour ⅔cup of the cooled, boiled water into the first three jars. Stir the mixture to dissolve the sugar. Do not pour water into the fourth jar. Put this jar away in a warm place.

4 Cut out pieces of plastic wrap about twice a jar's width. Stretch one across the neck of each remaining jar, and secure it with a rubber band. Put the first jar in a warm place.

5 Place the second jar in a glass bowl. Put some ice cubes and cold water into the bowl. This will keep the jar's temperature close to freezing.

6 Place the third jar in another glass bowl. Pour in some hot water that is almost too hot to touch. Be careful not to use boiling water, or the jar may crack.

high temperature

warm temperature

7 Regularly check all four jars over the next two hours. As the ice around the second jar melts, add more to keep the temperature low. Add more hot water to keep the third jar hot.

cold temperature

dry jar

In the jar that was kept hot, the yeast is a cloudy layer at the bottom, killed by the heat. The jar that was kept cold has only a little froth on the surface, because the cold has slowed down the yeast.

The yeast that was kept warm has fed on the water and sugar, and its gas is pushing up the plastic wrap. In the dry jar, there are no signs of activity, because the yeast is hibernating.

Preservation and decay

Decay is the breaking up of dead organic matter, such as animals and plants. It results when invisible creatures called bacteria, and tiny fungi called molds, breed. The bodies of living plants and animals fight these agents of destruction, but as soon as the animals die, decay begins. Bacteria and molds that cause decay need water to live, so decay happens best in damp conditions.

▲ **Protected by the gods**
Turning the body of a great Egyptian pharaoh into a mummy was a complicated process. In addition to the preserving process, a jackal-masked priest performed sacred rituals.

The process of preserving something aims to stop it from decaying. The ancient Egyptians were skilled at mummifying (preserving) their kings' bodies. They removed moist internal organs, such as the intestines, heart, liver, and brain. Then they buried the body in natron, a kind of salt. This dried out all the fluids that speed up decay. The body was then wrapped in bandages. The bandages had been soaked in oily resins that killed bacteria and moulds in a similar way to modern antiseptic creams. You can practice slowing down and speeding up the process of decay in these two experiments.

peeled carrot

unpeeled carrot

stone

plastic

unpeeled apple

peeled apple

wood

What decays?

1 Peel one of the apples and one of the carrots. Line the tray with some newspaper. Add a layer of soil mix and place all the items on top. Add more soil mix to cover the items.

2 Dig a shallow hole in a shady spot and put the tray in it. Cover it with soil so that you can just see its top edges. Buried like this, the items will stay damp. Dig the tray up after a week.

Examine the results. Fruit and vegetables are attacked quickly by bacteria and molds, especially if they have no skins. Wood takes months to decay. Stone and plastic do not decay.

Preventing decay

1 Put one slice of ordinary bread into a plastic bag, and seal it with a tie. Now toast another slice of bread until it is crispy and dry. Seal the toast in another plastic bag.

2 Spread some antiseptic cream, which is designed to kill germs, over one side of a third slice. Seal the antiseptic cream-coated third slice in another plastic bag.

3 Label each plastic bag. Leave them in a warm place and check them once a day. Bacteria and molds are everywhere. What will they do inside your plastic bags?

▲ Dry toast

Look at the slices. Mold and bacteria cannot grow on the dry toast, since there is no moisture.

Do not open the bags when you have finished looking at the results. Keep the molds and bacteria wrapped safely inside their plastic bags, and drop the bags into a garbage can.

▲ Antiseptic cream

The chemicals in the antiseptic cream have killed any germs on the cream-covered slice of bread.

▲ Ordinary bread

The ordinary slice of bread is very moldy. Mold and bacteria have thrived in the moist conditions.

Stone and concrete

Buildings that are made of hard stone last much longer than those made of dried earth or bricks. The people who lived in early civilizations carved stone with simple hammers and chisels—the same as you will try to do in the first experiment. When the ancient Egyptians built the pyramids more than 3,000 years ago, they had to drive large wedges into cracks in the rock face to lever off blocks of stone.

Ancient peoples used stone that they found locally, and gradually learned to use different rocks for different jobs. The Inca people of South America built with granite, a hard, igneous (volcanic) rock. The ancient Egyptians also used granite, but limestone, a softer, more easily carved sedimentary rock, was common too. Certain rocks, such as marble, were selected for decorative effects, because of their beautiful patterns and colors. Many modern buildings are made of concrete, a mixture of ground-down rocks and minerals. You can test its strength in the second experiment.

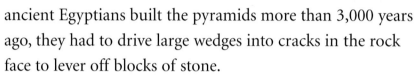

Nelson's Column · Sydney Opera House · Statue of Liberty · Great Pyramid, Giza

▲ **Ancient scale**
The Great Pyramid in Egypt is the largest stone building in the world, even though it was built over 4,000 years ago. It is made up of over 2 million blocks of stone, each of which weighs an average of 2½ tons.

YOU WILL NEED
blunt, round-ended knife, solid foam chunk used by flower-arrangers, foamed concrete (fairly soft) type of building brick.

Cutting and carving

1 Could you be a sculptor? Practice by marking out a simple shape on the flower-arranging foam. Use the knife to cut around it. How easy is it to use this material?

2 Now do the same with your building brick. This is much harder, but it is still softer than stone. Make sure that the knife blade is pointed away from you.

Now you know how hard it is to carve material that is much softer than stone. How long do you think it would take you to carve real stone with simple tools?

Mix your own concrete

1 Place one cupful of sand in a bucket. Add two cups of cement and a handful of gravel. Take care not to touch the cement with your bare hands.

2 Add some water to the mixture, little by little. Keep stirring all the time, until the mixture has the consistency of oatmeal. Mix it well with the stick.

3 Pour the wet concrete onto a shallow metal tray and spread it out. Leave it to solidify for about half an hour. Wash all the other equipment you have used right away.

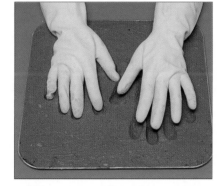

4 Now you can shape the concrete. Make impressions of your hands, or write with the stick. The marks will be permanent once the concrete has set. Do not use your bare hands.

hand prints in concrete

5 You could make a concrete brick like those used in the construction industry. Line a small, strong box with aluminum foil. Pour in the concrete and smooth the top with the stick.

How strong is the concrete brick once it has set? Test its strength by trying to bend it. Can you rest a heavy weight on top of the brick without breaking it?

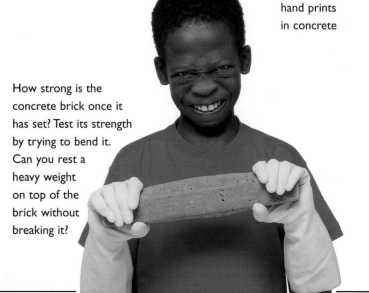

Building bridges

A platform bridge was a very early human invention, dating back tens of thousands of years. The simplest platform bridges were just a tree trunk or a single slab of stone, laid across a narrow river or steep gully, so that people could get across. Many modern platform bridges are hollow and made of steel. The model here shows how thin folded sheets make platform bridges stronger.

If you stand on a simple platform bridge, the downward force of your weight makes it sag in the middle. Too much weight can snap a flat wooden plank or crack a stone slab. As the second experiment shows, however, arch bridges do not sag when loaded. They curve up and over the gap that they span, and the forces acting on the arch squeeze it together. Weight from above is pushed outward, so that the load spreads to the side supports. The Romans were among the first to build arch bridges.

Make a platform

1 Cut out four strips of card 16 x 4in. With a ruler and pen, draw lines ½in apart across each card. Fold each card back and forth across the lines, to form zigzag pleats.

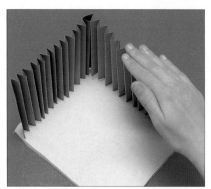

2 Lay one board flat on the table. Stand a piece of pleated card upright along the board's edges. Repeat for the other three sides. Use modeling clay to secure each corner.

3 When all sides of the platform are in place, lay the second board on top. Push downward with your hand. Pleating the card has made the platform very strong. Your platform is stronger than a platform bridge, because it is supported on four sides. Without this support, it would sag in the middle.

Make an arch

1 Although it is not shown in this picture, it would be a good idea to cover the work surface with newspaper first. Place the two bricks on the work surface about 8in apart.

2 Pile sand between the bricks, and smooth it with your hands to make a curved mound. Place the wooden blocks side by side across the sand. They should touch the outer blocks.

3 The inner blocks touch each other but have V-shaped gaps between them. Mix the plaster with water until it forms a stiff paste. Use the knife to fill gaps between the blocks with paste.

4 Make sure you have filled each space where the arch meets the bricks. Wait for the plaster to dry. Once it is dry, remove the sand from underneath the arch.

5 Push down on the arch and feel how firm it is. The weight that you are putting on the bridge is supported by the two bricks at the side. This bridge is stronger than a platform bridge, and does not sag in the middle. Like stone slabs in real bridges, the wooden toy blocks make a remarkably strong curve.

toy building blocks

Tunnel construction

Atunnel has to bear the weight of millions of tons of rocks and earth—or even water—above it. One way of doing this is to make lots of brick arches that together run the length of the tunnel. An arched roof is much stronger than a flat one, because weight from above is pushed out sideways, as the first experiment shows. In the second project, you place a wedge-shaped keystone at the peak of the arch. In real life, this keystone locks the whole structure together. It compresses (squeezes) the bricks on either side, to make the arch self-supporting and very strong.

Today, a long, trainlike machine is used to bore tunnels. A big drill carves out the hole, sending the waste backward on a conveyor belt. Behind it, robotic cranes lift precast concrete sections of the tube-shaped tunnel into place.

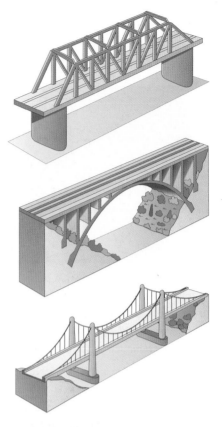

▲ Bridge types

The beam bridge (*top*) is made of horizontal platform supported on two or more piers (pillars). Arch bridges (*center*) are built over steep valleys and rivers. Suspension bridges (*bottom*) support the longest bridges. The weight of the platform is carried by steel wires that hang from cables. The cables are held up by concrete towers and anchored firmly at the valley's sides.

Templates

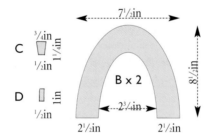

A x 2
10½in
13in
10½in

C
¾in
½in
1¼in

D
1in
½in

B x 2
7½in
8½in
2¾in
2½in
2½in

Strength test

YOU WILL NEED

two pieces of thick card (width roughly the same as the length of the blocks or bricks), two wooden building blocks or house bricks, a few heavy pebbles.

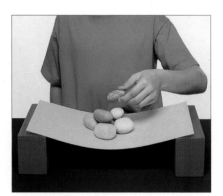

1 Place one of the pieces of card on top of the building blocks. Place pebbles on top as shown above. You will see that the tunnel roof sags under the weight.

2 Curve a second piece of card under the flat roof as shown. The roof supports the weight of the pebbles, because the arch supports the flat section, making it stronger.

Tunnel in a landscape

YOU WILL NEED

masking tape, two pieces of thick card measuring 14½ x 12in and 18½ x 10½in, ruler, pencil, scissors, thin card measuring 17¾ x 16in, newspaper, cup of flour, ½ cup of water, acrylic paints, paintbrush, water pot, thin card 8½ x 11in, white glue, glue brush, old sponge.

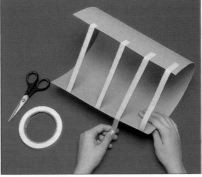

1 Tear off about four long strips of masking tape. Curve the 18½ x 10½in rectangle of cardboard lengthways. Use the tape to hold the curve in place as shown above.

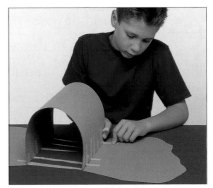

2 Copy the two templates A on to two 14½ x 12in pieces of thick card. Cut out the shapes. Attach each one to the sides of the tunnel, and secure with tape as shown above.

3 Fold the 17¾ x 16in thin card in half. Copy the arch template B onto the card. Cut out to make the two tunnel entrances. Stick these to the tunnel with masking tape as shown.

4 Scrunch newspaper into balls, and tape to the tunnel and landscape. Mix the flour and water to make a thick paste. Dip newspaper strips in the paste. Lay them over the tunnel.

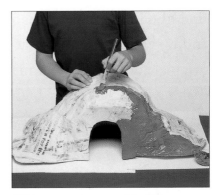

5 Leave to dry overnight. When completely dry and hard, paint the tunnel and landscape green. Apply up to three coats, letting each one dry before you apply the next.

6 Paint the thin card to look like brick. Draw and cut out templates C and D. Draw around them onto the brick card, to make the keystone and lots of bricks. Allow paint to dry.

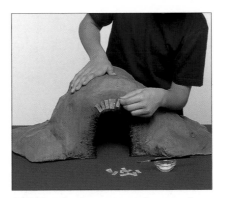

7 Glue the keystone at the top of the tunnel entrance. Then glue bricks around the arch at either side of the keystone. In real tunnels, there are keystones along the tunnel length.

8 Dip pieces of old sponge into green acrylic paint to make bushes. Leave to dry. Stick them on the landscape. Apply three coats of paint to the whole landscape.

The strength of a pyramid

Over a period of more than 4,500 years, people in different parts of the world built huge pyramids. The oldest Egyptian pyramids were started almost 4,600 years ago, while the most recent pyramids in Central America were finished about 600 years ago. Each one took a long time to build, sometimes over 50 years, and involved thousands of people.

Why did these civilizations opt for a pyramidal structure rather than a cube or a rectangle for their monuments? These experiments will help you to find out. In the first, by changing a cube into a pyramid, you end up with a structure that is three times taller than the original cube. A pyramid makes good use of material, by making the structure as high as possible. The second project shows that triangular shapes are more rigid than squares and do not collapse as easily. When an earthquake destroyed the Egyptian city of Cairo 700 years ago, the pyramids stood firm. Modern materials and technology make it possible to build tall, rectangular buildings that are strong and stable.

▲ **Steep challenge**

The Egyptians had no cranes to help them move the enormous slabs of stone used to build the pyramids. Workers built ramps of hard-packed earth. They hauled the slabs up these using plant-fiber ropes and wooden rollers. As the pyramid grew, the ramps became longer and steeper. When the pyramid was finished, the ramps were removed.

Bases and heights

1 Make two cubes from modelling material. The faces should measure about 1 or 1½in, but they must all be the same. Use a ruler to check your measurements.

2 Reshape one of the cubes to form a tall, square-based pyramid. Its base must be the same size as the original cube. You now have a cube and a pyramid.

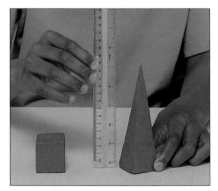

3 Now measure the cube and pyramid. They have the same volume and the same size base. The pyramid is three times taller, but is strong and more stable.

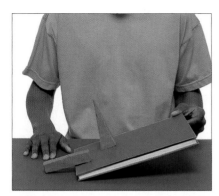

4 Make the cube into a long slabs. Place the slab and the pyramid on a book. Slowly tilt the book, to imitate the effect of an earthquake. The slab topples over before the pyramid does.

5 Make another smaller cube and pyramid from modeling material. Make sure that they are the same height. Their bases must also be the same size.

6 Do the same book test with the two smaller shapes. You should still find that the pyramid is the more stable of the two shapes. It is the second of the two shapes to fall over.

A question of strength

YOU WILL NEED

Bases and heights: nonhardening modeling material, plastic modeling knife, ruler, book.

A question of strength:
20 large, plastic drinking straws, reusable adhesive.

1 For this project, you will need two models—a cube and a square-based pyramid. Make them out of large plastic drinking straws and reusable adhesive. First, make the cube.

2 After fixing four straws to make the base of your cube, you need eight more to finish it. Make sure that your cube is even, with each face the same size.

3 Now make a square-based pyramid. The base should be the same size as the base of your cube. Make the base, and just fix four more straws to it to complete your pyramid.

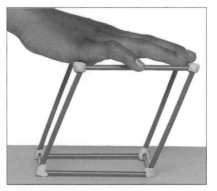

4 Push down gently with your hand over the center of the cube. Move your hand slightly to one side as you push down, and you will feel the cube start to collapse.

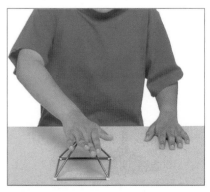

5 Repeat this with the pyramid. You can feel how much more rigid this shape is, and it does not collapse. This is because a pyramid has triangular-shaped faces that meet at a central point.

Surveying a site

Making precise measurements in order to put up a building is called surveying. Accurate building requires two things. There must be a level base to the building, and building slabs must be laid absolutely flat, with their sides perfectly vertical, at right angles to the ground. Builders use plumb lines to check that verticals are absolutely true. A plumb line is a weight on the end of a line, which holds the line straight. These experiments show how to use water levels or a plumb line to measure differences in heights on a site.

▲ **The lie of the land**
A modern surveyor makes a detailed examination of the land before building work can start.

Is it vertical?

1 Make your own plumb line by fixing a 1¼in ball of modeling material to a piece of string. Make a large knot in the string and model the material around it.

2 Push your stick into the ground. Make it as vertical as possible (pointing straight upward). Keep moving it slightly, until you are sure it is straight.

3 Now use your plumb line to check how straight your stick is. Get a friend to hold the line next to the stick. Measure between the stick and line at the top and farther down. If the measurements are the same, your stick is vertical.

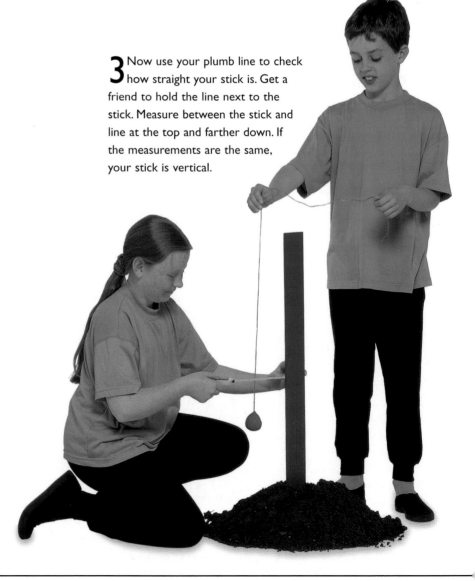

Is your site level?

YOU WILL NEED

Is it vertical?: nonhardening modeling material, string, a stick (about 1 yard long), tape measure.

Is your site level?: wooden stick 1 yard long, plank of wood 16 x 4in, nails, hammer, screw-in hooks, clear plastic piping (about ½in diameter), pitcher, water colored with ink, funnel, tape measure, wooden pole 1 yard long, pen.

1 Here, you are making a simple version of a surveyor's level. To start, nail the short plank of wood to the top of the long wooden stick. Take care with the hammer.

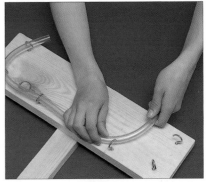

2 Now screw the hooks in along the bottom and up the sides of the plank. Thread the piping through the hooks. About ¾in of piping should stick up above the plank.

3 Get a friend to hold the device upright. Now, very carefully, pour the water into the pipe, using a funnel. The water level should come just above the piece of wood.

4 The friend holds the pole up 5 yards away. You look along the water levels so they line up, and also line up with the pole. The friend moves a finger up and down the pole. Shout when the friend's finger lines up with the water levels.

5 The friend marks this on the pole, then moves to another spot. Repeat step 4. The distance between the two marks on the pole shows the difference in level between the two places.

Powerful levers

One of the simplest and oldest gadgets in the world is the lever. Any rod or stick can act as a lever, helping to move heavy objects or prise things apart. Levers are also used for lifting, cutting, and squashing. The action of a lever can make a push more forceful, or make it a smaller push. It can also change the direction of a push. The difference between the size of the push you make on a lever (the effort) and the push the lever itself makes (the load) is called mechanical advantage.

A lever on a central pivot can also be used as a balance. The lever balances if the effect of the force (push) on one side of the pivot is the same as the effect of the force on the other. A seesaw is one sort of balancing lever. It is a plank balanced on a central post or pivot. A big person can balance someone small and light if they sit nearer to the central pivot of the seesaw.

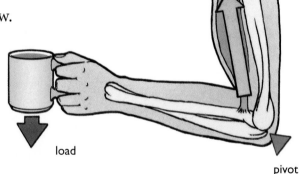

▲ Using a simple lever

A spoon can be a lever. This girl is using the spoon as a simple lever to lift the lid off a can of paint. The lever arm pivots on the lip of the can. As the girl pushes down on the long end, the shorter end wedged under the lid lifts it up with greater force, making the stiff lid move.

▲ Cracking a nut

The strong crushing action of the nutcracker's jaws is produced by pressing the two lever arms together. A pair of nutcrackers, like a pair of scissors or a pair of pliers, has two lever arms joined at a pivot. The levers make the effort you use about four times bigger, allowing you to break the nut easily. Putting the pivot at the end of the nutcracker rather than toward the center (as in a pair of scissors), means that the arms of the cracker can be shorter, but still create a force just as big.

lever arm

jaws

pivot

effort

load

pivot

▲ Body levers

Did you know that some parts of your body are levers? Every time you brush your hair or get up from a chair, the bones in your arms and legs act as levers. As your arm lifts up an object, your elbow is the pivot. Effort from the upper arm is transferred to your lower arm, so that you can pick up the load in your hand.

Levers and lifting

1 A ruler can be used as a lever to lift a book. With the pivot (the box) near the book, only a small effort is needed to lift the book up. The lever makes the push greater.

2 When the pivot is moved to the middle of the lever, the effort needed to lift the book up is equal to the book's weight. The effort and the load are the same.

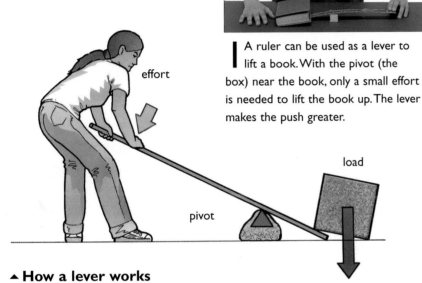

effort

load

pivot

▲ How a lever works

A lever tilts on a pivot, which is nearer to the end of the lever with the load on it. The effort, or force, is the push you make on the long end of the lever to lift the weight of the load.

3 When the pivot is near where you are pressing, more effort is needed to lift the book. The force of the push needed to lift the book is now larger than the book's weight.

Balancing a seesaw

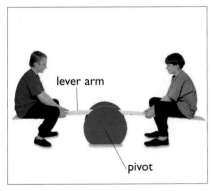

lever arm

pivot

1 Ask a friend of equal weight to sit on one side of the seesaw, while you sit on the other side. If you sit the same distance from the pivot, you make the seesaw balance.

2 Ask another friend to join you on the seesaw. By adding another person, that side of the seesaw will overbalance. The pair's greater weight will easily lift the lighter person.

3 Get the pair to move nearer to the pivot of the seesaw. Their weight can be balanced by the lighter person moving farther away from the pivot. The seesaw will be equally balanced.

Levers at work

Find out how to make three different kinds of lever in these experiments. The first is a can crusher that uses a lever action to squash a can. The second is a gripper for picking up small objects, just like a pair of tweezers. It can also work as a nutcracker. In a pair of nutcrackers, the load (in this case a candy or a nut) is between the pivot (the pencil) and the effort (where you push). In a pair of tweezers, the effort is between the pivot and the load.

The third experiment is a balance scale. It is like the ones used by the Romans about 2,000 years ago. It works by balancing the weight of an object against a known weight, in this case a bag of coins. The coins are moved along the lever arm, until they balance the object being weighed. The farther away from the pivot the weighed bag is, the greater turning effect it has on the lever arm. The heavier the weight being measured, the farther away the bag must be moved to balance the arm. The weight is read against the scale along the arm.

Can crusher

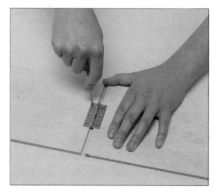

1 Lay the two planks of wood end to end. Ask an adult to help you screw them together with a hinge, using screws and a screwdriver. Make sure the hinge is secure.

2 Glue a jar lid to the inside edge of each plank of wood, with the top of the lid face down. The lids should be about halfway along each plank and the same distance from the hinge.

To crush a can, put the can in between the lids, so that it is held in place. Press down hard on the top piece of wood.

24

Gripper

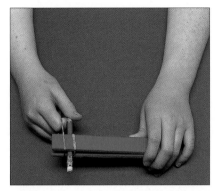

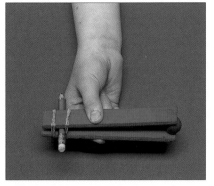

1 Put the pencil between the two pieces of wood, near one end. Wrap the rubber bands tightly around the pieces of wood to make a pivot. You have now made the gripper.

2 Hold the gripper near the pivot to make it act like a pair of tweezers. See if you can pick up a delicate object, such as a candy or a grape, without crushing the object.

3 Hold the gripper at the end farthest away from the pivot. Now your lever operates as a pair of nutcrackers. The effort at the point you push is increased.

Balance scale

YOU WILL NEED

Gripper: short pencil, two pieces of wood each about 6in long, thick rubber bands, objects to pick up or squash, such as candies or nuts.

Balance scale: thick card about 20 x 3in, thin card, scissors, string, ruler, hole punch, 4½in circle of card, tape, 4oz of coins, felt-tipped pen, objects to weigh.

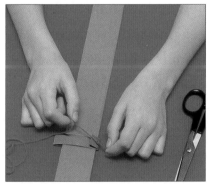

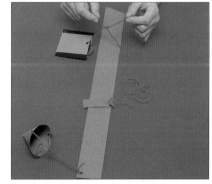

1 Make the arm by folding the thick card in two. Make a loop of thin card and fold it loosely around the arm 4¼in from one end. Tie a piece of string to this support.

2 Make a hole ½in from the arm's end. Make the card circle into a cone. Tie it to the hole. Make an envelope from thin card, and tie it to a loop so that it hangs over the arm.

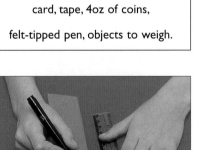

3 Put the coins in the envelope and seal it up. Starting from the middle of the support, make a mark every 2in along the arm. This scale will tell you the weight of an object.

To weigh an object, put it in the cone and slide the envelope of coins backward and forward along the arm, until the arm balances. Each mark along the scale equals 2oz. In this picture, the object being weighed is about 3oz.

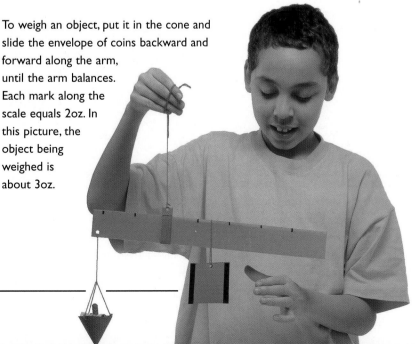

25

The power of energy

Nothing can happen without energy. Energy is needed to do work, such as making things move. To make something move, a source of energy is needed. For example, an engine works by burning fuel—a storage of chemical energy. The two experiments here explore different ways in which energy can be captured to make something move.

The turbine experiment shows how the energy in flowing water makes a bottle spin. This energy is used in hydroelectric power stations to generate electricity. The second project shows how electrical energy from a battery spins a motor. Electric motors are used in many household appliances, such as vacuum cleaners and washing machines.

The development of the steam engine and the electric motor in the 1800s provided new sources of energy that were able to power ships and railway engines, for example, and later, to light homes and streets.

▲ **Strike a light**
Lightning is a massive discharge of energy from a thundercloud. The cloud gets overloaded with electrically charged particles of water and ice.

YOU WILL NEED

scissors, plastic bottle, pencil, two wide drinking straws, plastic tape, thin string, tray, water.

3 Hold your turbine over a tray, or outdoors, so that you will not make a mess with the water. Fill the bottle with water. It will squirt out through the straws, making the bottle spin.

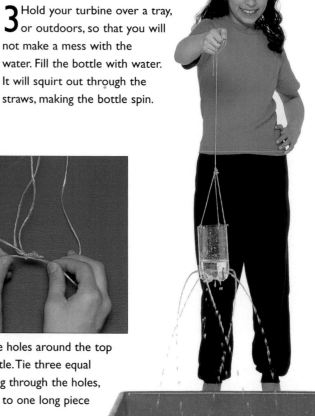

Turbine

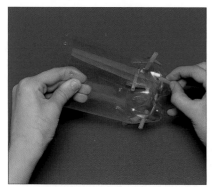

1 Cut off the bottle's top. Use the pencil to poke holes around its base. Cut the straws and push them through the holes. Use tape to hold the straws in place.

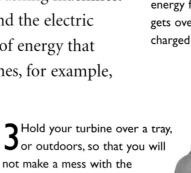

2 Poke three holes around the top of the bottle. Tie three equal pieces of string through the holes, and join them to one long piece of string.

Electric motor

YOU WILL NEED

bradawl, two (red) end supports 2 x 2in, ruler, glue for plastic, (blue) plastic modeling board 6 x 4 x ¼in, scissors, drinking straw, two (yellow) coil supports 2½ x 2in, two (white) coil support spacers 1½ x 1in, wire strippers, insulated (plastic coated) copper wire, thread reel, aluminum foil, thin tape, knitting needle 6in long, two (green) magnet supports 1¼in high, two powerful bar magnets, four paper clips, two flexible connecting wires 8in long, thick plastic tape, 6-volt battery.

1 Use the bradawl to make a hole ½in from the top of each of the two end supports. Glue them to the base board, ½in inward from the shorter edges.

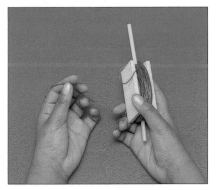

3 Strip ¾in of insulation from one end of the wire and 1¼in from the other. Wind wire between the coil supports. Slide the reel onto the straw, with the longest part of the straw showing.

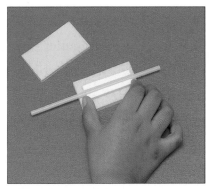

2 Cut a length of straw 4½in long. Glue the straw to one coil support. Glue the two coil support spacers to either side of the straw. Glue the second support over the top.

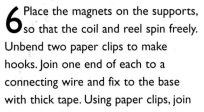

6 Place the magnets on the supports, so that the coil and reel spin freely. Unbend two paper clips to make hooks. Join one end of each to a connecting wire and fix to the base with thick tape. Using paper clips, join the ends of the wires to the battery. The reel should start spinning around.

4 Cut a foil strip the width of the reel, to fit three-quarters of the way around the reel. Cut it in half. Put the wire ends against the reel. Tape foil over each wire so it is under the foil's center.

5 Stick the reel to the straw. Hold it between the end supports. Slide the knitting needle through the hole in each end support. Secure the coil support with green magnet supports.

Wind and water power

Modern windmills called wind turbines are used to generate electricity. The most efficient wind turbines only have two or three blades, like the propeller of an aircraft. Sometimes just a couple of large turbines can generate enough electricity to meet all the power needs of a small community.

There are several shapes of wind turbine. One of the most efficient is the vertical-axis type. This has an axle like the dowel one in the first project. It is very efficient, because it works no matter which way the wind is blowing. The second experiment shows you how to make a water wheel that captures the energy of falling water to lift a small weight. Pour water from different heights to see if it makes a difference to the wheel's speed.

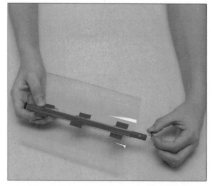

sails   simple gears

grinding stones

▲ Wind for milling

A windmill uses the power of the wind to turn heavy mill stones that grind grain to make flour. The whole building can be turned around, so that it faces into the wind. The speed of the mill is controlled by opening and closing slots in the sails. Inside a windmill is an arrangement of gear wheels, which transfers power from the sails to the grinding stones.

YOU WILL NEED

plastic bottle, scissors, tape, ruler, thin dowel, thumb tacks.

Make a windmill

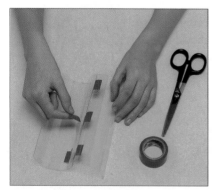

1 Cut the top and bottom off the bottle to leave a tube. Cut the tube in half lengthwise, then stick the two halves together in an S shape, so that the edges overlap by ¾in.

2 The piece of dowel should be about 1½in longer than the vanes. Slide it into the slot between the vanes. Press a thumb tack gently into each end of the dowel.

To make the windmill spin, hold it vertically with your fingers on the thumb tacks at each end of the dowel. Blow on the vanes. The windmill will spin easily.

Make a water-wheel

1 Cut the top third off the plastic bottle. Cut a small hole in the bottom piece near the base (this is to let the water out). Cut a V-shape on each side of the rim.

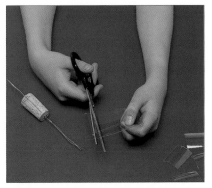

2 Ask an adult to push the wire through the center of the cork to make an axle. From the top third of the plastic bottle, cut six small curved vanes (blades) as shown.

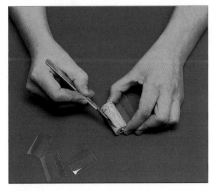

3 Ask an adult to cut six slots in the cork with a craft knife. (This might be easier without the wire.) Push the plastic vanes into the slots to make the water wheel.

5 Put the water wheel on a large plate or in the sink. Pour water onto the wheel, so that it hits the upward-curving vanes. As the wheel turns, the weight should be lifted up.

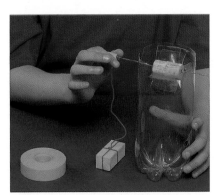

4 Rest the wheel's axle in the V-shaped slots. Tape a piece of string toward one end of the axle, and tie a small weight to the end of the string. Fill a pitcher with water.

Energy from liquid and air

Hydraulic machines have parts that are moved by liquid. Pneumatic machines have parts that are moved by a gas such as air. A hydraulic system has a pipe filled with a liquid, such as oil, and a piston that moves to and fro within the pipe. Pushing liquid into the pipe forces the piston to move, transmitting power from one end of the pipe to the other. In a simple pneumatic system, compressed air forces a piston to move.

In the first experiment, you make a simple hydraulic machine powered by water pressure. Water is poured from a central reservoir (the pitcher of water) into a pipe. The water fills up a plastic bag. The bag expands and forces up the piston (the lid), which in turn raises a heavy object. Many cranes and trucks use this principle to lift heavy loads. In the air pump project, you discover the basic principles of how vacuum cleaners work. Finally, you make a miniature vacuum cleaner. Air is sucked in one hole and pushed out of another. A valve stops it from being sucked in and pushed out of the wrong holes.

◄ **Filling an empty space**
Modern vacuum cleaners have an air pump operated by an electric motor. The pump creates a vacuum inside the cleaner. Dust rushes in from the outside to fill the vacuum.

YOU WILL NEED

large plastic bottle, scissors, airtight plastic bag, plastic tube, tape, plastic funnel, spray can lid, heavy book, pitcher of water.

Make a hydraulic lifter

1 Cut the top off the large plastic bottle. Make sure the plastic bag is airtight, and wrap its neck over the end of a piece of plastic tube. Seal the bag to the tube with tape.

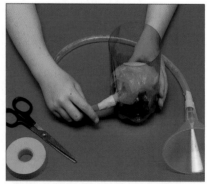

2 Fix a funnel to the other end of the tube. Make a hole at the base of the bottle, and feed the bag and tube through. The bag should sit in the bottom of the bottle.

3 Put the spray can lid on top of the bag, and rest a heavy book on top of the bottle. Lift the funnel end of the tube up, and slowly pour in water. What happens to the lid and the book?

Make an air pump

1 Cut around the large plastic bottle, about one third up from the bottom. Cut a slit down the side of the bottom part of the bottle, so that it will slide inside the top part.

2 Ask an adult to help you nail the bottom of the bottle to the end of a wooden stick or a piece of dowel. You have now made a piston for your air pump.

3 Cut a hole about ½in across near the neck of the bottle. Cut a piece of card about ¾ x ¾in. Tape one edge of the card to the bottle to form a flap over the hole.

4 Drop a ping-pong ball into the top part of the bottle, so that it rests in the neck. Push the bottom part of the bottle (the piston) into the top part (the cylinder).

5 Move the piston in and out, to suck air into the bottle and out of the hole. Can you see how both the valves work? The flap should automatically close when you pull the piston out.

Make a vacuum cleaner

1 Make the air pump from the project above without the card flap. Tape string to the ball, feed it through the bottle's neck, and tape it down, so that the ball is held near the neck.

2 Make a tissue paper bag and glue it over the hole near the neck of the bottle. Air from the pump will go through the bag, and anything the vacuum picks up should be trapped.

3 Try picking up tiny bits of paper with the vacuum. Pull the piston out sharply to suck the bits of paper into the bottle. Push the piston back in gently to pump the paper into the bag.

How magnets work

Magnets are usually made of the metal iron, or another material that has lots of iron in it, such as steel. Magnets can be various shapes, but all of them have the ability to pull things toward themselves. This invisible force is called magnetism. Magnets only attract (pull) metals that are made of iron or that contain iron.

Magnetism is concentrated around the poles (ends) of a magnet. A magnet has two poles, called the north pole and the south pole. The two poles may look the same but they behave differently. Put one pole of a magnet near to a pole of another magnet, and watch what happens. You may feel an attraction (pulling) force as the two poles stick together. Alternatively, you may feel a repulsion (pushing) force, as the two poles push away from each other. In all magnets, identical poles will repel (push away) each other, while different poles will pull towards each other.

Is a big magnet more powerful than a small one? Not always. You cannot tell how powerful a magnet is just by looking at it. Compare the strength and power of different magnets in the projects opposite.

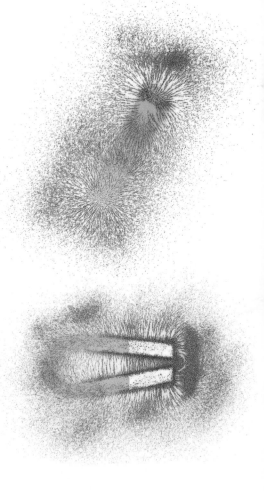

Tiny magnets ▶
Think of a bar of iron as having millions of micromagnets inside it. These are called domains. If they are all jumbled up, the bar is not a magnet. If the micromagnets in a bar are lined up and point the same way, it is a magnet.

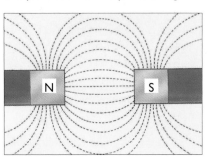

◀ Attraction and repulsion ▶
The poles of two magnets that are different or opposite will attract. Magnetic lines of force from north and south poles pull together and join. The poles of two magnets that are the same will repel or push each other apart.

▲ Seeing magnetism
You cannot see the magnetic force around a magnet, but you can see the effects of its presence when an iron nail sticks to a magnet. You can see the shape of a magnetic field by using tiny, powderlike pieces of iron, called iron filings. Iron filings reveal that the lines and strength of the magnetic force are concentrated around and between the poles at the end of the horseshoe magnet. On a bar magnet, they line up to show how the magnetic force spreads out from the poles (ends).

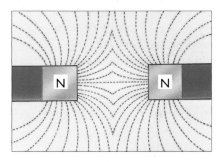

Strength of a magnet

1 Cut off a piece of tape and use it to tape the round container firmly to the work surface. The round container will act as the pivot, or the balancer.

2 Attach a magnet to one end of the ruler with a rubber band and some washers to the other end of the ruler. Position the middle of the ruler on the balancer.

3 Hold another magnet above the first. Lower it until the ruler tips over. Measure its height above the table. The higher it is when the ruler tips over, the stronger the magnet.

YOU WILL NEED

Strength of a magnet: scissors, tape, round plastic container, two magnets, ruler, rubber bands, steel washers.

Power of a magnet: pencil, thumb tacks, strong thread, card, ruler with holes at both ends and in the middle, scissors, tape, rubber bands, adhesive dots, pen, two small bar magnets.

Power of a magnet

1 Attach one end of a piece of thread to a tack and the other to a pencil. Draw two large quarter-circles on card. The distance from the pin to curved edge should be as long as the ruler.

2 Draw a triangle in one quarter-circle and cut it out. Using the triangle as a template, cut out a triangle from the other quarter-circle. Tape them together.

3 Push a tack through the ruler's end hole, so that it pivots. Attach rubber bands from the ruler's middle hole to the quarter-circle's side. Add dots labeled N and S to each ruler end.

Stand the magnet measurer upright. Attach one magnet to the ruler's top end with a rubber band. Bring the unlike pole of another magnet near it. How far can it pull the ruler? Stronger magnets pull it farther.

Magnetic Earth

The Earth behaves as if there is a giant bar magnet running through its middle from pole to pole. This affects every magnetic material that comes within its reach. If you hold a magnet so that it can rotate freely, it always ends up with one end pointing to the Earth's North Pole and the other to the South Pole. This is how a compass works—the needle automatically swings to the North. The Earth's magnetism comes from its inner core of iron and nickel.

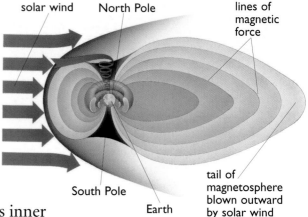

solar wind North Pole lines of magnetic force

South Pole Earth tail of magnetosphere blown outward by solar wind

You can use the compass you make here to plot a magnetic field like the Earth's. The Earth's magnetic field is slightly tilted, so compasses do not swing exactly toward the North Pole, but to a point a little way off from northern Canada. This direction is known as magnetic north.

Make a compass

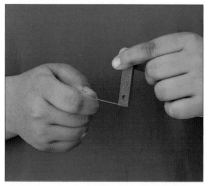

1 To turn the needle into a magnet, stroke the end of the magnet slowly along it. Repeat this in the same direction for about 45 seconds. This magnetizes the needle.

▲ Magnetic protection

The effects of Earth's magnetism extend 37,000 miles out into space. In fact, there is a vast magnetic force field around the Earth called the magnetosphere. This traps electrically charged particles and so protects the Earth from the solar wind—the deadly stream of charged particles hurtling from the Sun.

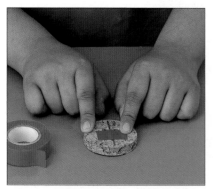

2 Place the magnetized needle on the slice of cork. Make sure that it is exactly in the middle, otherwise it will not spin evenly. Tape the needle into place.

3 Fill the bowl nearly to the brim with water, and float the cork in it. Make sure the cork is exactly in the middle and can turn without rubbing on the edges of the bowl.

The Earth's magnetic field should now swivel the needle on the cork. One end of the needle will always point to the north. That end is its north pole.

Magnetic field

YOU WILL NEED

Make a compass: steel needle, bar magnet, slice of cork, tape, small bowl, water.

Magnetic field: large sheet of paper, bar magnet, your needle compass from the first project, pencil.

1 Lay a large sheet of paper on a table. Put the magnet in the middle of the paper. Set up your needle compass an inch or two away from one end of the magnet.

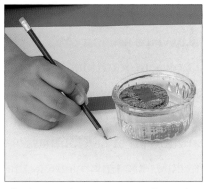

2 Wait as the compass needle settles in a particular direction as it is swiveled by the magnet. Make a pencil mark on the paper to show which way it is pointing.

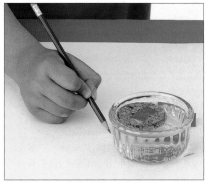

3 Move the compass a little way toward the other end of the magnet. Mark a line on the paper to show which way the needle is pointing now.

4 Repeat Step 3 for about 25 different positions around the magnet. Try the compass both near the magnet and farther away. You should now have a pattern of marks.

Look at the pattern of marks you have made on the paper. They should form a series of rings around the magnet, like layers of an onion. Earth's magnetic field is shaped like this.

35

Magnets and maps

Look at a map—which way up does it go? Maps are important. They let us know our location. Without magnets, we would not know how to use a map or find our way around an area. Compass needles are tiny magnets that rotate to point to the Earth's magnetic north. Look on a local map to find a diagram of the compass points, an arrow, or 'N' that indicates north. Then set a compass so that the needle points north. Turn the map so that its north faces the same way as the compass north. Now the map is lined up accurately in relation to the landscape. If you are on a hilltop with wide views, you can see how the map is a tiny plan of the countryside around.

▲ Magnetic migration

The yellow arrows show the migration routes of the Arctic tern. The routes follow the Earth's magnetic force. The tern flies from north to south and then, later in the year, from south to north. Birds may also use rivers, mountains, coastlines, the Sun, Moon, and stars to help them find their way.

▲ Which way up? ▶

We are so familiar with maps having north at the top, that they look odd when they are turned around. Can you recognize this country (*top*) when it is turned upside down? Can you find it on the globe (*right*)?

Loop compass

1 Straighten out a paper clip. Magnetize it by stroking it with the strong magnet. Cut a disk of card, bend the wire into a large loop, and insert it into holes in the card.

2 Tape the paper clip to the piece of cork and to the card circle. Tie the thread to the top of the wire loop. Let it hang and twirl around freely. It is now ready to test.

3 Does the paper clip magnet work as a compass needle and point north and south? Check it with the store-bought compass. What do you find happens?

Drawing a maze

YOU WILL NEED

Loop compass: paper clip, strong magnet, card, scissors, thin wire, tape, cork tile, thread, store-bought compass.

Drawing a maze: cardboard, colored pens, compass.

1 Draw a maze on cardboard. Make it colorful and fun. Put in some dead ends and false turns. Make sure one route leads all the way through from one end of the maze to another!

2 Record your course through the maze, using compass points for the direction. You can limit the information to north, south, east, and west or include northeast, southwest and so on.

Can you find your way through this maze? When you have made it to the other side, try recording your route with compass points. At the beginning of the journey, you head east, turn north and then go east again. Can you complete these instructions for the entire journey?

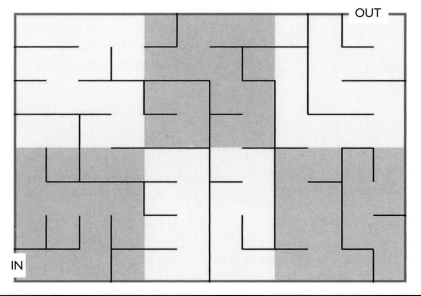

Electric magnets

Some magnets, such as bar and horseshoe magnets, are permanent. They have what scientists call "spontaneous permanent magnetism." Their magnetism needs no outside force or energy to create it. A way of making magnetism is by using electricity. When electricity flows through a wire or another similar conducting (carrying) material, it produces a magnetic field around the wire. This is called electromagnetism or EM. In fact, magnetism and electricity are very closely linked. Each can be used to make the other. EM is used in many tools, machines, and devices. Some electromagnetic machines use the electricity from batteries. Others need the much more powerful mains electricity from wall sockets.

The first practical electromagnets were made by the British bootmaker and spare-time scientist, William Sturgeon. He used them to amaze audiences at his science shows in the 1820s. The basic design has hardly changed since. You can make a similar electromagnet in the projects.

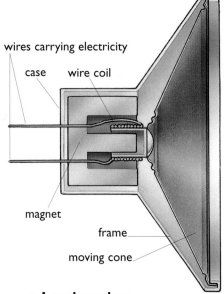

wires carrying electricity
case   wire coil
magnet
frame
moving cone

▲ Loudspeaker
Electrical signals are transferred to the loudspeaker along a connecting wire (speaker lead). Electricity flows through the wire coil, which is attached to the plastic speaker cone. The signals make the coil into an electromagnet that varies in strength. This magnetic field is itself inside the field of a strong permanent magnet. The two fields interact, with like poles repelling. This makes the coil move or vibrate, and the loudspeaker cone vibrates, too. This in turn sends out sound waves.

▸ Creating a magnetic field
As electricity flows through a wire, a magnetic field is created around it. The magnetic lines of force flow in circles around the wire. This is called an electromagnetic field. As soon as the electricity is switched off, the magnetism stops.

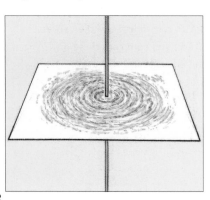

◂ Seeing electromagnetism
If iron filings are sprinkled onto a piece of cardboard that has an electricity-carrying wire through it, the filings are affected by the magnetic field. They arrange themselves in circles to show the lines of magnetic force, as they do with an ordinary magnet.

▾ Are you receiving me?
The earpiece of a telephone receives varying electrical signals from the mouthpiece of the telephone held at other end of the line. The earpiece works like a simple loudspeaker to recreate the sounds of the speaking person's voice.

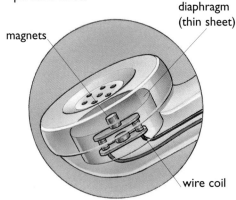

diaphragm (thin sheet)
magnets
wire coil

Electromagnet

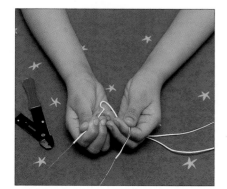

I Using the wire strippers, carefully remove an inch or two of plastic insulation from each end of the wire. These bare ends will connect to the battery.

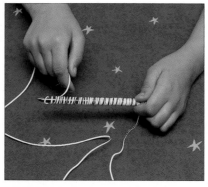

2 Carefully wrap the wire into a tight coil around the iron nail. The plastic insulation around the wire conducts the electricity around the iron nail.

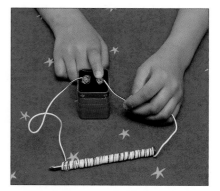

3 Connect the wire's ends to the battery terminals. (It does not matter which is positive or negative.) Test your electromagnet by picking up paper clips.

Adding a switch

```
YOU WILL NEED

Electromagnet: wire strippers, 2
yards of wire (insulated, plastic-
coated, multistrand copper), large
iron nail, 9-volt battery, paper clips.
Adding a switch: hole punch
piece of card, brass fasteners.
```

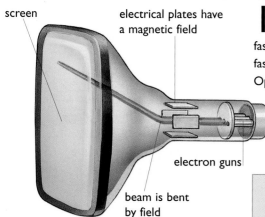

screen

electrical plates have a magnetic field

electron guns

beam is bent by field

I Make two equal-sized holes in the piece of card. Push the brass fasteners into them. Push one of the fasteners through a paper clip first. Open out the legs of the fasteners.

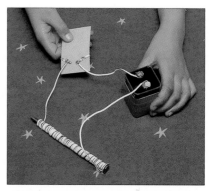

2 Connect one end of electromagnet wire to the fastener. Connect the other to a battery terminal. Attach the remaining fastener to the other terminal with short wire. Turn the card over.

▲ Inside a television

Television sets, computer monitors, and other similar screens have electromagnet-type devices inside. These are usually shaped like flat plates. They bend the beam that scans across the screen line by line, to build up the picture. This occurs many times every second.

```
WARNING!
NEVER use electricity from wall
sockets. It is too dangerous and
could kill you. Ask an adult for help
with this project.
```

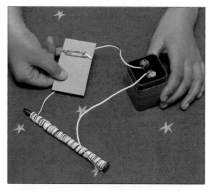

3 Push the paper clip attached to one fastener away from the other fastener. No electricity flows. Turn the clip to touch the fastener. Electricity flows, switching on the electromagnet.

Computer data storage

The hard disk of a computer consists of a number of flat, circular plates. Each one of these plates is coated with tiny magnetic particles. The hard disk also contains a controlling mechanism called the read/write head. This is positioned slightly above the magnetic plates. Data (information) is sent to the disk as a series of electrical pulses. These are sent to the read/write head, which contains a tiny electromagnet. The head magnetizes the tiny magnetic particles on the surface of the plates. This pattern of particles on the disk represents the data. You can see how this happens in the project.

When reading information, the magnetized particles on the hard disk create a small current in the head as the plates spin under it. This is then converted by circuits into binary code, a number system that computers use. The code is based on just two numbers (binary means two), 0 and 1. Different combinations represent the letters of the alphabet.

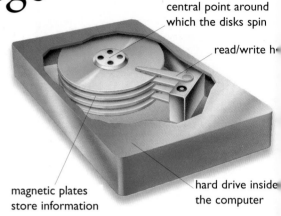

central point around which the disks spin

read/write head

magnetic plates store information

hard drive inside the computer

▲ Inside the hard drive

A typical drive consists of a stack of thin disks, called a platter. The upper surface of each disk is coated with tiny magnetic particles, and each disk has its own read/write head on a movable arm. When storing and reading information, the disks spin at very high speeds (up to 100 revolutions a second).

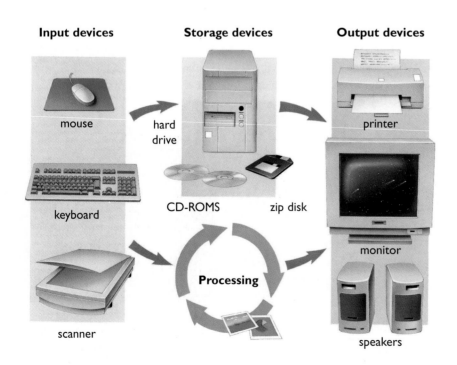

Input devices

mouse

keyboard

scanner

Storage devices

hard drive

CD-ROMS

zip disk

Processing

Output devices

printer

monitor

speakers

◀ Using computers

When people use a computer, they are doing four different things:

1. Inputting data (information) using an input device.

2. Storing the data so that it can be reused (often called data storage).

3. Working with the data they put in (often called processing).

4. Retrieving and looking at the data using an output device.

Storing data on disk

1 Draw a circle with a diameter of 8in on the piece of white card. Draw three more circles inside, each with a diameter ¾in smaller than the one before. Cut out the largest circle.

2 Position a ruler at the center of the circle where the compass point has made a hole. Draw four lines through the middle to divide the circle into eight equal parts.

3 Use a red marker to color in six or seven sections as shown above. Leave the remaining section white. The white areas represent full disk space. Red areas are empty disk space.

4 Attach some modeling material to the rim of a plastic cup. Then turn it upside down on a smooth surface. Press it down gently to make sure it is secure. Place the disk on top.

5 Push the thumb tack through the middle of the disk into the cup. Make sure the disk can turn. Scatter paper clips on the surface. Hold the magnet under the disk. Move it around.

The paper clips will move around the surface of the disk, and all line up in one section of the disk. This is what happens to the magnetic particles on a hard disk when an electric current is passed through them by the read/write head. In a computer, the way the magnetic particles line up is a record of the data stored on the hard disk. Remove the paper clips from the disk. Spin the disk clockwise with one hand, and with a finger of the other hand, touch areas of the disk. If you stop the disk on a white part, you have found data. If you stop on a red section, you have found empty disk space.

Magnet sports

Y̶ou can make your own table-top car race, using some magnets. Small, flat, bar and ring magnets are best. The trick is to stay on the track and speed along, but not so fast that the magnet loses your car! If that happens, the race is over. The second project shows you how to create your own Olympic Games using an electromagnet. A washer represents a discus; a nut, a shot put; a nail, a javelin. Use the electromagnet to throw each of them. When you switch off the electromagnet, it releases the iron or the steel object.

Magnetic racing

1 Carefully glue a magnet to the end of each ruler or strip of wood. Use 12in rulers if you can, or if these are unavailable, use similar-sized strips of wood.

2 Draw the shapes of some racing cars on the colored card. You can make the wheels a different color and maybe add stripes, too, so that each car looks different.

3 Carefully cut out the racing car shapes with scissors. Decorate the cars with stick-on shapes, such as stars, to make up your own racing team.

4 Glue a steel paper clip to the underside of each racing car. Let the glue dry thoroughly while you draw a racing track on a large sheet of cardboard.

Put the track on two books, so it is raised all around the edges. Place your racing cars on the start line. Push the ruler underneath, so the magnet faces upward and attracts the paper clip on the base of your car. Move the ruler slowly, so the magnet drags the paper clip and car along. Practice driving like this for a while before you race your opponent.

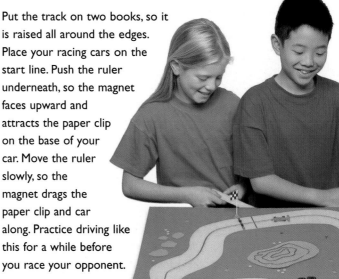

Electromagnetic Olympics

1 Cut a sheet of card into a base about 20 x 16in. Cut four strips the same length and 4–6in. deep, for the sides. Glue the sides and base together.

2 Cut out squares of card for the scoreboard, and tape them together to make a sheet that will fit neatly into the box. Write numbers on them and decorate them.

3 Fit the scoreboard into the box. It is best not to glue it, since you may wish to take it out and change the scores, or make a new scoreboard as you become an expert at the games.

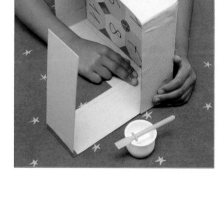

4 Cut two more card strips. Tape them together at each of their short edges. Glue the other short edges inside the box, on opposite sides. Position this "arch" at one end of the box.

5 Make an electromagnet from the nail and wire. Tape it to the arch, so it hangs below by its wires. Connect the free ends of the wire to the battery. Use a paper clip as a battery switch.

Push the nail that hangs below the wires to test that it swings back and forth. Switch on the nail electromagnet using the paper clip switch. It should attract an iron or steel object, such as the nail, which is the javelin. Push the nail electromagnet so it swings back and forth. Turn off the switch, and the javelin will be released. Note where this lands on the scoreboard.

Images from light

The picture on a television screen is made up of thin lines of light. In the first project, you will see that a television picture is made up from rows of glowing dots of colored light. The picture consists of just three colors—red, green, and blue. Viewed from a distance, these colours mix to produce the full range of colors that we see naturally around us—as the second experiment demonstrates.

Fax machines work in a similar way to television, only more slowly. When you feed a sheet of paper into a fax machine, a beam of light moves back and forth across it. Dark places absorb the light, and pale places reflect it. The reflected light enters a detector that produces an electric current. The electric current is changed into a code made up of chirping sounds. These travel down the line to the receiving fax machine. This code controls a scanner that moves across heat-sensitive paper and produces a facsimile (copy) of the original. The final project shows how a fax machine breaks an image into tiny squares that are black and white.

screen

cathode ray t

electron beam

▲ Cathode ray tube
The cathode ray tube is the heart of a television. Pictures are received in the form of electrical impulses. These impulses control a stream of electrons inside the cathode ray tube. The electron beam scans across the screen and creates the pictures as points of colored light. This is the picture that the viewer sees.

TV screen

YOU WILL NEED

TV screen: TV set, flashlight, powerful magnifying glass.

Secondary colours: red, green, and blue transparent plastic sheet, 3 powerful flashlights, 3 rubber bands, black card.

Digital images: ruler, pencil, tracing paper, photograph, black felt-tipped pen.

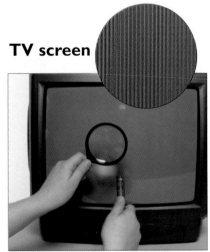

1 Turn off the TV. Shine the flashlight close to the screen and look through the magnifying glass. You will see that the screen is covered in very fine lines.

2 Turn on the TV and view the screen through the lens. The picture is made up of minute rectangles of light colored red, green, and blue.

Secondary colors

1 Attach a piece of colored plastic over the end of each of your three flashlights. Stretch the plastic tightly, and use a rubber band to hold it firmly in place.

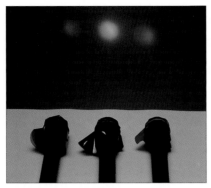

2 Shine the flashlights onto the black card. You can see the three different primary colors of red, green, and blue.

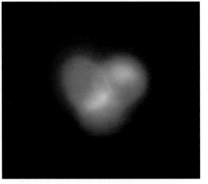

3 Position the flashlights so that the three circles of colored light overlap in a clover leaf pattern. Overlapping colors mix to give new, secondary colors.

Digital images

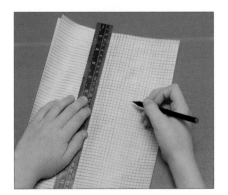

1 Draw lines ¼in apart to cover the tracing paper in squares. Put the paper over the photograph. Use the pen to fill each dark square. Leave each light square blank.

The picture is made from squares that are either black or white.

The result is a "digitized" image, which means it can be represented by numbers—the digit 1 for white squares, and the digit 0 for black squares. The digitized image contains less detail than the original photo. You could increase the detail of the image by using a greater number of smaller squares.

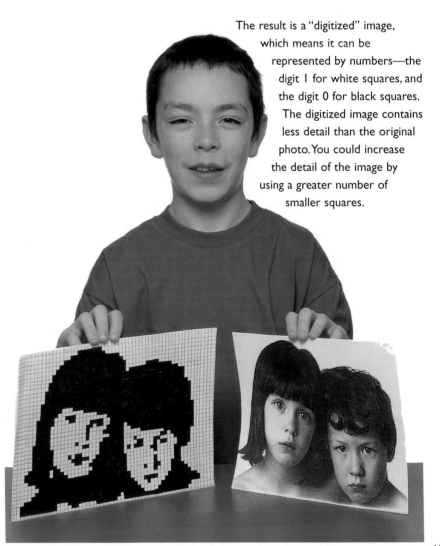

Cameras and light

What is the vital piece of equipment you must not forget if you are on vacation or having a birthday party? Your camera! To most people, a camera is simply a device for taking snapshots of their favorite people and places. In fact, modern cameras are sophisticated light-recording machines that make use of the very latest breakthroughs in technology and computer science.

Cameras work in a similar way to your eyes, but they make a permanent record of a scene that you can share with other people. They record scenes on film, or digitally by collecting light from that scene and turning it into a picture. Although light appears to be white, it is actually made up of light of many colors like a rainbow. The first experiment shows you how to break the light spectrum into its component parts by shining light through water.

Cameras have three basic parts. The camera body holds the film. The shutter opens to allow light to come through to the lens. The lens bends rays of light and directs them onto the film to make a picture. In the second experiment, you can collect light from a scene to make a picture, in the same way that a camera works.

Split light into a rainbow

1 Carefully lean the mirror against the inner side of the dish. Use two pieces of reusable adhesive to stick both sides of the mirror to the dish at an angle as shown.

2 Pour water into the dish until it is about 1½in in depth. Notice that as you fill the dish, a wedge-shaped volume of water is created alongside the mirror.

3 Switch on the flashlight. Shine the beam from the flashlight onto the surface of the water in front of the mirror. This should produce a spectrum or "rainbow."

4 In dim light, hold up the piece of white card above the dish to look at your rainbow. You may need to alter the positions of the card and flashlight before you can see it properly.

Make your own viewer

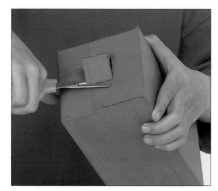

1 Use a pair of sharp scissors to cut a small square hole, approximately ¾ x ¾in, in one end of the cardboard box. You may need an adult's help to do this.

2 Now cut a much larger square hole in the other end of your cardboard box. Cut out most of the end of the box, as shown in the picture.

3 Cut a square of thin card about 1½ x 1½in. Find the center of the card using a ruler. Use a sharp pencil to pierce a tiny hole in the center of the card.

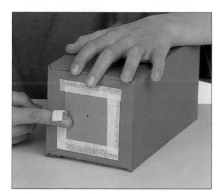

4 Place the piece of thin card over the outside of the smaller hole on the box. Make sure that the pencil hole is centerd over the square hole. Now tape it into place.

6 Look out of a window, through the screen of tracing paper. Try tracing the image you see onto the paper.

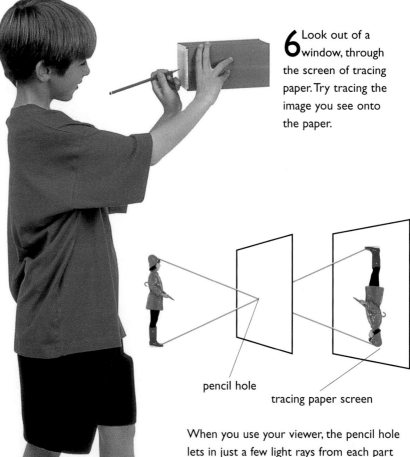

pencil hole

tracing paper screen

When you use your viewer, the pencil hole lets in just a few light rays from each part of the scene. The rays keep going in straight lines and hit the tracing paper screen, making an upside-down image of the scene.

5 Cut a square of tracing paper slightly bigger than the larger hole at the other end of the box. Stick it securely over that hole. Your viewer is now ready to use.

A photographic image

The camera's job is to create a focused image of a scene, but this would be no use without a way of recording the image. This is the job of the film. There are three basic types of film—color negative, color-reversal, and black and white. Film comes in different sizes (called formats) and lengths. Most cameras take 35mm film, and the usual lengths are 24 and 36 exposures.

Film is coated with chemicals that are affected by light. When an image strikes the film, the coating records the patterns of light, dark, and color. Film has to be developed with chemicals before you can see the recorded pictures. Until then, it must be kept in complete darkness. When undeveloped film is exposed to direct light, it turns black.

This project shows that you do not need to have a camera to see how film works. In fact, you do not even need a film! You can use black and white photographic paper instead. Photographic paper is the paper that prints are made on. It works in the same way as film. Here, you can see how to make a picture called a photogram. It is made by covering some parts of a sheet of photographic paper with objects and then shining light on the sheet. When the paper is developed, the areas that were hit by the light turn black, leaving you an image of the objects.

YOU WILL NEED

developer for paper (not film) and fixer (both from a photographic supplier), rubber gloves, protective glasses, plastic dishes, desk lamp, photographic paper, different-shaped objects, such as keys and scissors, plastic tongs.

▲ **Danger!**
This symbol, on photographic chemical bottles, means that they can be dangerous if not used with care. Always wear protective gloves and goggles.

◀ **Photographic paper**
For black and white prints, you need a paper called monochrome paper. Buy the smallest size you can, and choose grade 2 if possible, with a gloss (shiny) finish. The paper comes in a light-proof envelope or box. Only open the envelope in complete darkness. The paper is in a second, black polyurethene envelope. You will also need two photographic chemicals—developer for paper (not film) and fixer. Buy them from a photographic supplier, and ask an adult to help you use them safely.

Make your own photogram

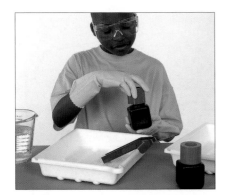

1 Ask an adult to help you follow the instructions to dilute the chemicals with water. Protect your eyes and hands when handling them. Store the diluted chemicals in plastic bottles.

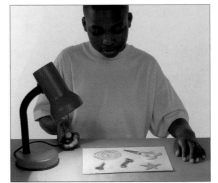

2 Turn off the lamp. Lay a sheet of photographic paper down, shiny side up. Put some objects on it. Then turn the lamp on again for a few seconds.

3 Pick up the paper with the tongs, and put it into the dish of developer. Push the paper down, so that it is completely underneath the liquid.

4 After a minute, use the tongs to move the paper into the fixer. Leave the paper right under the liquid for a minute, until the image is fixed.

images made on photographic paper

5 Now you can turn the light back on. Using the tongs, lift the paper out of the fixer and wash it with running water for a few minutes. Then lay the paper on a flat surface to dry. This technique is an excellent way of producing unique invitations and greetings cards quickly and effectively.

Getting in focus

Before taking a photograph, you need to make sure that your subject is in focus. When it is, all the rays of light that leave a point on the subject are bent by the lens, so that they hit the correct place on the film. This makes a clear, sharp image. Parts of the scene inside or behind the subject may not be in focus. On some cameras, you have to choose the part of the scene that you want to be in focus. Autofocus cameras focus the lens by automatically choosing the object at the center of the image to be taken.

This experiment involves making a simple camera with just a few basic pieces of equipment. It uses photographic paper (paper with a light-sensitive coating on one side) instead of film, and a pinhole instead of a lens. When the paper is processed, you will have a negative. The "Easy prints" project on the next page shows you how to develop it.

viewfinder

lens pentaprism

light ray mirror

▲ Focusing SLRs

With an SLR (single lens reflex) camera, you can see exactly what the image looks like through the viewfinder. On a manual-focus SLR, you turn a ring around the lens until your subject comes into focus. When the subject is in focus, the light rays meet on the film focal plane. This is the exposed part of the film that is held flat at the back of the camera by a pressure plate. You can see it if you open the back of your camera when it is empty.

YOU WILL NEED

pinhole box viewer, aluminum foil,

scissors, tape, pencil, black paper,

thin card, ruler, heavy light-proof

cloth or plastic sheet, photographic

paper, rubber band.

◀ Get it sharp

In this photograph (*left*), the subject is in sharp focus. You can see all the fine detail. When the same shot is out of focus (*below*), it makes the subject look blurred. Autofocus cameras focus on the object in the middle of the viewfinder and do the job of focusing for you.

Making a pinhole camera

1 Make the pinhole viewer from the earlier "Make your own viewer" project, but remove the tracing-paper screen. Replace the 1½in card square with aluminum foil.

2 Pierce a hole, about ¹⁄₁₆in across, in the middle of the foil using a sharp pencil. Open the back of the box. Roll up some black paper, and fit it through the large hole to line the inside.

3 Cut a square of card large enough to cover the aluminum foil. Tape just the top edge of the square of card to the box, so that it will act as a shutter.

4 Measure and cut a square of card to fit across the other end of the box. Tape it to one edge, so that it closes over the hole like a door or flap.

5 Lay the heavy, light-proof cloth or light-proof plastic sheet on the working surface. Cut a piece of the cloth or sheet large enough to fold around the end of the box.

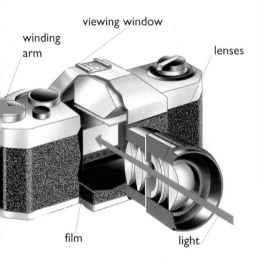

winding arm

viewing window

lenses

film

light

▲ Reflex action

In a single lens reflex camera, light enters through the lenses at the front and strikes the film at the back. Users can see clearly what they are photographing by means of a prism mounted in the camera.

6 In a completely dark room, and feeling with your fingers, put a piece of the photographic paper underneath the flap at the end of the box.

7 Close the flap, then, still feeling with your fingers, wrap the cloth or plastic sheet tightly over it. Next, put a rubber band tightly around the box to secure it.

8 Now you can turn the light on. Point the camera at a well-lit object and open the shutter. Leave the camera perfectly still for about five minutes, and then close the shutter.

Letting in the light

Exposure is the word for the amount of light that reaches the film in your camera. The aperture (opening) is a hole behind the lens that can be adjusted to let more or less light on the film. Changing the aperture affects both the brightness of an image and the depth of field that is in focus. Your eyes work in the same way. If the light is bright, your pupils get smaller to protect your retinas. If the light is dim, then the pupils enlarge to let in more light. In the experiment opposite you can investigate different apertures for yourself.

One of the first things photographers want to do is to get their films developed, so that they can see how the pictures have turned out. If you have just taken a photograph with the pinhole camera you made in an earlier project, you can find out how easy it is to turn it into a photographic print in the project below.

YOU WILL NEED

Easy prints: photographic paper and chemicals, negative from pin-hole camera, flashlight or desk lamp, safety glasses, rubber gloves, plastic dishes, plastic tongs or tweezers. **Amazing apertures:** magnifying glass, cardboard tube, tape, scissors, thin card, tracing paper, desk lamp.

▲ **How does a shutter work?**
Open the back of your camera (when there is no film inside). Place a small strip of tracing paper where your film usually goes. Aim the camera at a subject and press the shutter release button. You should see a brief flash of the image on your tracing paper.

Easy prints

1 In a totally dark room, lay a fresh sheet of photographic paper on a flat surface, shiny side up. Lay the negative from your pinhole camera face down on top.

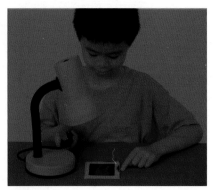

2 Shine a flashlight or a desk lamp on the top of the two papers for a few seconds. Turn the light off, and remove your paper negative. Put on the safety glasses and gloves.

3 Put the fresh paper into a tray of developing fluid, then fix and wash the paper (see the earlier project, "Make your own photogram"). You should end up with a print of the original image.

Amazing apertures

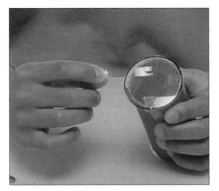

1 Make sure that your magnifying glass fits into your cardboard tube. Then carefully attach the magnifying glass to one end of the tube using small pieces of tape.

2 Roll a piece of thin card around the other end of the cardboard tube. Tape the top edge down so that it makes another tube that slides on and off the first one.

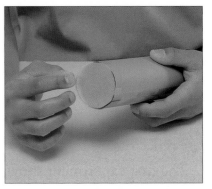

3 Cut out a circle of tracing paper with a diameter the same as the sliding card tube. Use tape to attach it across the end of the tube. This will form your viewing screen.

4 With the viewing screen facing toward you, aim your tube at a desk lamp that is turned on. Can you see an image of the bulb on the screen?

5 Slide the tubes slowly together, until the image of the bulb is clear and in focus. Now adjust the tubes again so that the image is slightly out of focus.

6 Cut a hole (about ¼in wide) in a piece of card, to make a small aperture. Look at the light bulb again and hold the card in front of the lens. The smaller aperture will bring the light bulb into focus. Is it clearer? Can you read the writing on the bulb?

How telescopes work

Optical telescopes use lenses or mirrors to make distant objects look bigger and brighter. Lens telescopes are also called refractors. Mirror telescopes are called reflectors. Most large astronomical telescopes for looking at stars are reflectors.

The first experiment shows you how to make a reflecting telescope, using a mirror. A reflecting telescope's main mirror is curved, so that light rays bounce off at an angle.

The refracting telescope in the second experiment uses lenses. There are difficulties involved in making big lenses, which is why most of the telescopes used in astronomy are reflectors. Our brains work out how big an object is by analyzing the angle of the light rays from it as the rays enter our eyes. Telescopes use lenses or mirrors to change this angle. Bending light rays from distant objects makes them seem larger than they would appear to the naked eye.

YOU WILL NEED

desk lamp, thick purple paper, marker pen, scissors, tape, small mirror, nonhardening modeling material, magnifying glass.

eyepiece lens

starlight

primary mirror reflects an upside-down image

secondary mirror corrects image

▲ Reflecting telescope

Light reflects off the primary mirror. The light rays bounce off a small secondary mirror, and are focused and magnified by an eyepiece lens. Astronomers use telescopes to help them study the stars and other planets. Telescopes are often built on top of mountains, for the clearest views. There, the air is thin and there are no lights from towns. The William Herschel Telescope (WHT) is located 8,000ft above sea level on top of an extinct volcano on La Palma, in the Canary Islands.

Make a single-mirror reflecting telescope

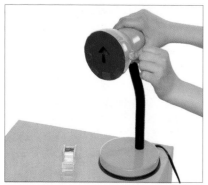

1 Draw a circle around the front of the desk lamp on a sheet of purple paper. Cut it out. Then cut out an arrow in the middle. Stick the circle onto the front of the lamp.

2 Set up the desk lamp and mirror so that the mirror reflects the light from the lamp onto a nearby wall. Use modeling material to help support the mirror, if necessary.

3 Set up the magnifying glass, so that light reflecting from the mirror passes through it. The lens magnifies and focuses the light, projecting an upside-down arrow.

Make a refracting telescope

YOU WILL NEED

desk lamp, thick red paper, marker pen, scissors, tape, two magnifying glasses, nonhardening modeling material.

1 Draw around the front of the desk lamp on a sheet of red paper. Using scissors, cut out a star in the middle of the circle. Then cut out the circle, as shown.

2 Using tape, fasten the circle of paper securely over the front of the desk lamp. Make sure that it does not touch the bulb, because this could cause the paper to burn.

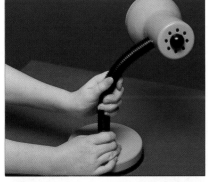

3 Position the desk lamp so that it shines on a nearby wall. Adjust the angle of the lamp if necessary. Make sure that the lamp's base is stable, to prevent it from tipping over.

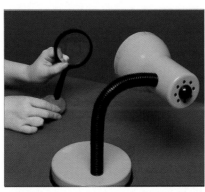

4 Position a magnifying glass between the lamp and the wall. To support the glass and fix it in place, take the handle and wedge it firmly in a lump of modeling material.

5 Turn on the lamp. Adjust the magnifying glass, so that the light passing through it appears as a blurred patch of light on the wall. The glass acts like a telescope's objective lens.

6 Position the second lens behind the first lens. This acts as an eyepiece lens. Adjust the eyepiece lens, until the light is focused to form the sharp image of the star.

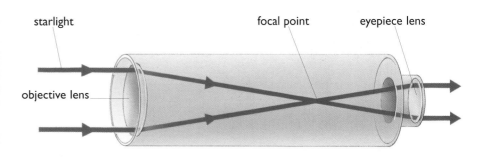

starlight   focal point   eyepiece lens

objective lens

▲ Refracting telescope

Light from a distant star passes through the objective lens. The light rays from distant objects change direction as they enter the lens, and again as they leave it. A magnified, blurry image of the star appears. The image is brought into focus by the lens in the eyepiece.

Satellites and orbits

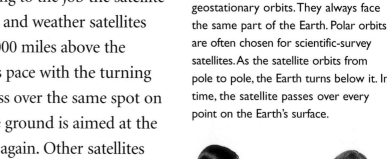

The movement of a satellite around the Earth is fixed in either a circular or an elliptical (oval) orbit. The satellite can be positioned in a polar orbit, circling the Earth from pole to pole, or placed in an equatorial orbit around the Equator, or in any orbit in between. It may cross the sky several times a day in a low Earth orbit (LEO), or it may hang in one place, in geostationary orbit. In the first project you can see for yourself how geostationary orbits work.

The type of orbit is chosen according to the job the satellite is there to do. Most communications and weather satellites are placed in geostationary orbit 22,000 miles above the Equator. A satellite in this orbit keeps pace with the turning Earth, and appears to hang motionless over the same spot on the ground. Once a radio dish on the ground is aimed at the satellite, the dish need not be moved again. Other satellites have to be tracked using movable radio dishes that follow the satellite as it crosses the sky. The second project demonstrates the way in which satellites relay signals from one place to another.

▲ Types of orbits

Weather satellites are often placed in geostationary orbits. They always face the same part of the Earth. Polar orbits are often chosen for scientific-survey satellites. As the satellite orbits from pole to pole, the Earth turns below it. In time, the satellite passes over every point on the Earth's surface.

YOU WILL NEED

about 15 strips of blue card, about 30 strips of red card, rope, a friend.

Geostationary orbit

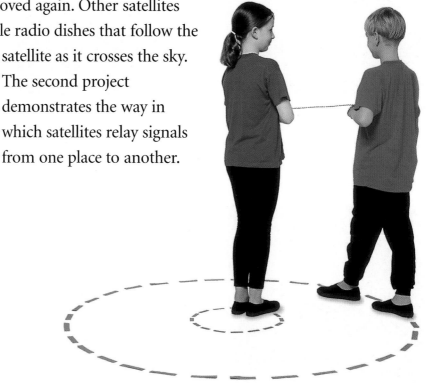

| Use the card strips to mark a blue circle, with a larger red circle around it on the ground. Hold one end of the rope, and ask a friend to hold the other end.

2 Walk around the inner circle, while your friend walks around the outer circle. The blue inner circle represents the Earth, and the outer circle represents the orbit of a satellite around the Earth. If your orbiting friend keeps pace with you as you walk, your human satellite is in a geostationary orbit.

Make a satellite relay

YOU WILL NEED

scissors, blue paper, tin can,
tape, 1 yardstick, thin card,
flat mirror, nonhardening
modeling material, flashlight.

1 Using the scissors, cut out a rectangle of blue paper just big enough to wrap around the tin can. Tape it in place. The tin can will act as a ground-based radio receiver.

2 Measure out a 4 x 4in piece of card with the ruler. Cut it out and stick it to one side of the tin can. This will act as an antenna on your tin-can receiver.

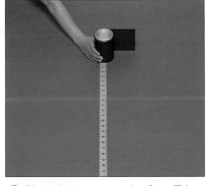

3 Place the tin can on the floor. Take the yardstick and lay it on the floor directly in front of the tin can. Place it on the opposite side to the antenna, as shown.

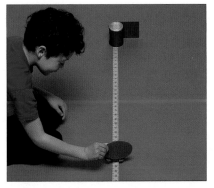

4 Place the mirror on the ruler about 2½ft from the tin can. The mirror will act like a satellite in geostationary orbit relaying signals. Fix in place with modeling material.

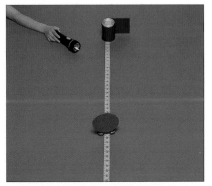

5 Darken the room. Place the flashlight beside the can, as shown. The flashlight will send out light beams in the same way that a ground-based transmitter sends out radio waves.

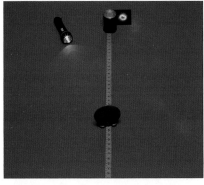

6 Switch on the flashlight. Move the mirror along the yardstick. Keep moving it, until the light beams are reflected off the mirror satellite and onto the antenna of the tin can.

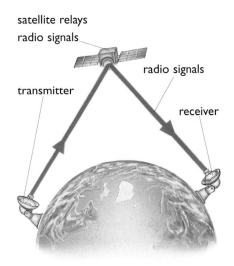

satellite relays radio signals

radio signals

transmitter

receiver

◄ Redirecting radio waves
Comsats (communication satellites) in geostationary orbit above the Equator allow radio transmissions to be sent to anywhere on the Earth's surface. Radio signals are transmitted from one side of the planet, and aimed at the orbiting satellite. The comsat then relays (redirects) the signal to a receiver on the opposite side of the Earth.

Power boost in Space

Some space probes, including *Pioneer 10* and *11*, used gravity boosts to help them travel through the Solar System. To get a boost, a probe passes by a planet and becomes attracted by its gravity. It is pulled by the planet on its orbit around the Sun. Some of the planet's orbital speed is transferred to the probe, which is then catapulted toward the next planet to be visited. This slingshot effect is vital, as robot spacecraft would not be able to carry enough fuel to change course from planet to planet. The first project shows how the slingshot effect works. Space probes send back information to Earth by radio signals. These are collected by large dish antennae on Earth. The second project shows why many of the radio antennae used are dish-shaped.

▼ Pioneering probes
Probes have landed on or flown past almost every planet in the Solar System. The most widely traveled deep space probes are *Pioneer 10* and *11*, and *Voyager 1* and *2*, which have toured most of the Solar System's outer planets. They used the pull of gravity from each planet they passed to change their course and send them to the next planet. *Pioneer 10* flew past Jupiter, and the flight path of the *Pioneer 11* probe took it past Jupiter and then to Saturn.

YOU WILL NEED

two thick books (of equal thickness), 24 x 12in piece of thick card, marble-sized steel ball, strong magnet, tape, two 12in lengths of wooden dowel.

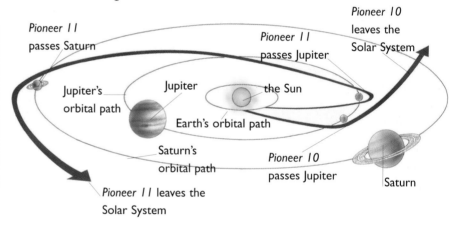

Pioneer 11 passes Saturn

Pioneer 11 passes Jupiter

Pioneer 10 leaves the Solar System

Jupiter's orbital path

Jupiter

the Sun

Earth's orbital path

Saturn's orbital path

Pioneer 10 passes Jupiter

Saturn

Pioneer 11 leaves the Solar System

Gravity boost

1 Place the books flat on a table about 6in apart. Lay the piece of card on top of the books, then roll the steel-ball space probe across it. It moves smoothly across the surface.

2 Place the magnet under the card. Roll the steel-ball probe across the card. It is drawn toward the magnet planet by the gravitylike pull of its magnetic field.

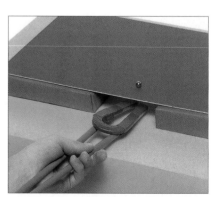

3 Tape the magnet to the dowel. Roll the ball and then pull the magnet away. The ball speeds up and is pulled along by the magnet planet, like a probe getting a gravity boost.

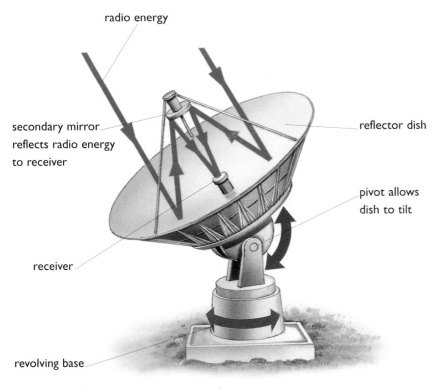

radio energy

secondary mirror
reflects radio energy
to receiver

reflector dish

pivot allows
dish to tilt

receiver

revolving base

◄ Beaming waves

Dish antennae reflect their collected radio energy back to the receiver. Space probes use their antennae to receive radio signals from mission control on Earth. The receiver can also act as a transmitter, allowing the probe to send back its findings to Earth.

YOU WILL NEED

plain postcard, pencil, ruler, scissors,

2 x 3ft piece of thick card,

nonhardening modeling material,

8 x 20in strip of mirror

board, flashlight.

Make a dish antenna

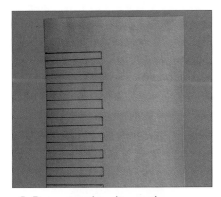

1 Draw nine thin slits on the postcard using the pencil and ruler. Each slit should measure 1 x ¼in. They should be equally spaced out from each other, ¼in apart.

2 Using the scissors, carefully cut out the slits in the postcard. The slits in the card will filter light, splitting it up into thin rays that will reflect off the curve of the antenna.

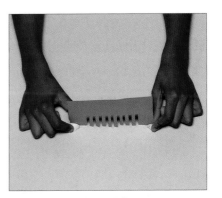

3 Place the large piece of thick card on a table. Stand the postcard 16in from one end of the card, with the slits facing down. Fix it in position with modeling material.

4 Bend the reflective mirror board to form a semicircular antenna, as shown. Stand it at one end of the thick card base. Then fix it firmly in position using modeling material.

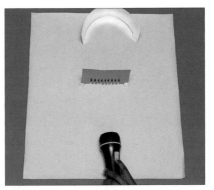

5 Switch on the flashlight. Direct the light beam, so that it shines through the slits in the postcard. The light is split into thin rays, which reflect off the mirror board.

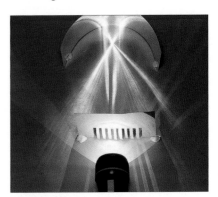

6 Darken the room. Move the flashlight until the light rays reflecting off the curved mirror are brought together at one spot, like radio waves on a dish antenna.

Listen to this

Sound is energy that moves back and forth through the air in the form of vibrations. These vibrations spread outward as waves, like the ripples caused by a stone when it is dropped into rather still water.

The first experiment demonstrates the existence and energy of sound waves. Channeling the sound inside a tube concentrates the waves in the direction of the tube. By channeling sound toward a candle, you can use the energy to blow out the flame.

The second experiment is all about the strength of sound waves. It shows that sounds get quieter if their waves are allowed to spread out. Scientists say that loud sounds have large amplitudes (areas of range).

In the final project, you can investigate pitch, or the range of sounds, by making a set of panpipes. Low sounds consist of a small number of vibrations every second. Musicians describe these sounds as having "low pitch" but scientists report the sounds as "low frequency." The panpipes show that pitch depends on the length of each pipe.

▲ **Play it again, Sam!**
You can play deep, low notes on a bass guitar. The sound waves vibrate slowly with a frequency as low as 50 times each second. High notes vibrate much more rapidly.

How sound travels

1 Stretch the plastic wrap tightly over the end of the tube. Use the band to fasten it in place. You could also use a flat piece of rubber cut from a balloon instead of the plastic wrap.

2 Ask an adult to light the candle. Point the tube at the candle, with the open end 4in from the flame. Give the plastic wrap a sharp tap with the flat of your hand.

You will hear the sound coming out of the tube. It consists of pressure waves in the air. The tube concentrates the sound waves toward the candle flame and puts it out.

Sound waves

1 Place the watch close to your ear. You can hear a ticking sound coming from it. The sound becomes fainter when you move the watch away from your ear.

2 Place one end of the tube over a friend's ear, and hold the watch at the other end. The tube concentrates the sound and does not let it spread out. She can hear the watch clearly.

How to make panpipes

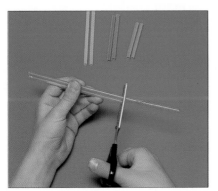

1 Cut the drinking straws so that you have four pairs that are 3½in, 3in, 2½in, and 2in long. Block up one end of each straw with a small piece of modeling material.

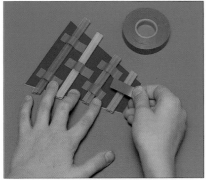

2 Carefully cut out the card to the same shape as the blue piece shown above. Fix the straws into place with the tape from long to short, to align with card as shown.

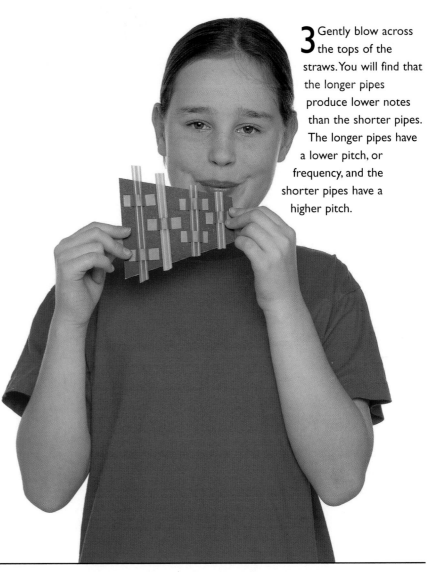

3 Gently blow across the tops of the straws. You will find that the longer pipes produce lower notes than the shorter pipes. The longer pipes have a lower pitch, or frequency, and the shorter pipes have a higher pitch.

Glossary

A

aerodynamics The way in which objects move through the air.
alloy A material, usually a metal, that is made from a mixture of other materials.
aperture A hole behind the lens of a camera, which can be adjusted to let more or less light on to the film.
APS (Advanced Photographic System) A camera that allows you to change the format of the photograph for individual shots.
autofocus A feature on cameras that automatically adjusts the position of the lens to ensure that a scene is in focus.

B

battery A container of chemicals that holds a charge of electricity.
binary code The digital code computers use, made up of two numbers, "0" and "1".

C

CAD Computer-aided design.
CD-ROM (compact disk read-only memory) A portable computer disk that stores information.
compass An instrument that contains a magnetized strip of metal, used for finding direction.

D

data Pieces of information.
database An organized store of information.
depth of field In photography, the range of distances within which a scene is in focus.
dish antenna A large, dish-shaped aerial used to receive signals in radar, radio telescopes, and satellite broadcasting.
disk drive The device that holds, reads, and writes on to a disk.

E

electricity A form of energy caused by the movement of electrons (charged particles) in atoms.

exposure time The time it takes for a camera to take a picture.
exposures Photographs on a film.

F

fax machine A machine that photocopies and electronically sends and receives written words and pictures over a telephone line.
focal plane The area at the back of a camera where the exposed film is held flat.
force A push or a pull.
friction The force caused by two surfaces rubbing together. This results in the slowing down of movement and heat being made.

G

gravity The pulling force that exists between large masses.

H

hard disk A computer's main storage disk, which holds the operating system.

hardware All the equipment that makes up a computer—disk drives, monitor, keyboard, mouse, etc.
hydraulics The use of water and other liquids to move devices such as pistons.

I

infrared Electromagnetic radiation with a wavelength between the red end of the visible spectrum, and microwaves and radio waves.
insulate To cover or protect something to reduce the amount of heat or electricity entering and/or leaving it.

J

jet propulsion Reactive movement to a jet of fluid or gas.

K

keystone The central stone in the arch of a bridge or curved part of a building.

L

lens An object made of a transparent material, such as glass, that is curved on one or both sides. It bends and directs beams of light to form or alter the view of an image.

lever A long bar that moves around a pivot to help move a heavy object.
lift The force generated by an airfoil that counters the force of gravity and keeps a flying object in the air.
light spectrum The colors that light can be split into.
lithosphere The rigid outer shell of the Earth, including the crust and the rigid upper part of the mantle.
load The weight moved by a lever or other machine.

M

magnetism An invisible force found in some elements, especially in iron, which causes pieces of iron to be either pushed apart or drawn together.
mass The amount of matter there is in a substance or object. Mass is measured in pounds, tons, etc.
monochrome Shades of black and white, with no other colors.
mummy An embalmed or preserved body.

N

negative In photography, the image on the developed film from which photographic prints are made. The colors in a negative are reversed, so that dark areas appear to be light and light areas appear to be dark.

O

orbit The curved path followed by a planet or other body around another planet or body.

P

pivot A central point around which something revolves or balances.
plastic A durable, synthetic material that is easily molded and shaped by heat.
plumb line A string with a weight at one end that is used to check whether a building is vertical.
primary colours Red, blue, and green (light), or magenta, cyan (blue), and yellow (pigment or solid color). These colors are the basis for all other shades and colors.
prism Specially shaped glass used to split white light into the spectrum, and to refract light rays away from their normal path.
propellant The fuel or force that causes something to go forward, such as the fuel in a rocket.
prototype The first working model of a machine from a specific design.

R

RAM (random access memory) The part of a computer memory that holds data temporarily until the computer is switched off.
reflecting telescope A telescope that uses mirrors.
refracting telescope A telescope that uses lenses.
refraction Bending of light rays.
ROM (read-only memory) Computer memory that holds information permanently.

S

satellite A celestial or artificial body that orbits around a planet or star.

shutter Camera mechanism that controls the amount of time light is allowed to fall on the lens.
software Applications found on computers that allow them to carry out specific tasks.
Solar system The family of planets, moons, and other bodies that orbit around the Sun.
sound wave Vibration moving through air or other substances which transmits sound.
space probe A spacecraft that works in deep space.
space shuttle A vehicle designed to be used for at least 100 space flights.
space station A large, artificial satellite in which astronauts live and work.
surveying To look at or examine a building or piece of land in detail to get a general view.

T

turbine A machine that generates power using gas, water or wind.

W

weightlessness A state in which an object has no actual weight, because it is not affected by gravity.

Index